In the pursuit of perspective

Zanika Mehta

Presentation by *BookLeaf Publishing*

Web: www.bookleafpub.com

E-mail: info@bookleafpub.com

ISBN: 9789357442282

First edition 2023

To my snowflake, forever and always.

ACKNOWLEDGEMENT

Thank you to my family for supporting me throughout my life.

PREFACE

Over my last few years of healing, there has been a few laws that I have encountered. This book is a compilation of those laws. They have helped me to reframe and reshape the way in which I navigate myself through this life. I hope it can help you too.

#1

In a moment, only temporary, you tasted like
forever.
The sound of your smile, the touch of your love;
forever.
It was in the loudness that I felt still.
It was in the silence that I felt consumed.
Maybe that was the problem.

Maybe over all these years, I have done nothing
but acquire a certain taste.
The kind that's sweet to the mouth, but bitter to
the heart.
Yet somehow, forever tasted so good, with you.

It was only until I realized that the taste of
forever you gave me, was just a sample.

You dipping your toes in,
Me living off the taste,
of forever,
in a moment only temporary.

#2

It really scares me how
We all can just pretend
Display an outward act
Then I guess that's just the end.

Reality is you're alone
With everything stuck inside your head

Law of duality states that
If you make peace with your pain
You can move forward
Maybe find your freedom again

That's the point of fear though
When it is at its worst
That's exactly when you
Have to dive head first

#3

Suffocating,
with your words wrapped around my neck.
Delusional,
with your thoughts stuck inside my head.
I sat frozen.
For hours, trying to find a way out.

Until it occurred to me.
The only way to get through this
Is to be more of myself, so

Take up space, I thought.

Protect the air that's left within you;
and dissolve the matter in its own water.

Fluidity.

#4

It's uncomfortable.
When it's time for things to grow;
Before,
You can sense it when it's time, things aren't
working anymore and that's the loudest.
During,
The pains of letting go, shedding skin,
perseverance throughout.
After,
Discovering & adjusting all within and all
without.
All of it, it's just uncomfortable.

The more you fight it
The louder it gets
And if that happens
You've lost the bet

You're an investment and growth is worth the
discomfort; bet on yourself.

#5

5

I can be nothing to you
If I am nothing for myself, first.

#6 Contradiction

6

People are afraid to live, more than they are
afraid to die. But behave the opposite.
Most die before they actually live.
But, the solution is in the contradiction.

#7 Truth

7

Truth forces accountability.

#8 Peace

8

Peace = the overlap between accepting who you
are and knowing what you are not.

#9 Forgiveness

9

Self-forgiveness and forgiveness create the gateway to freedom. Because it is the only way to claim back what is yours and let go of what is not.

#10 Fear

10

Fear of the unknown in life is the root of
self-limitation

#11 Love

11

Love is not what you do, love is who you are.

#12 Humility

12

The highest form of self-esteem is humility.

#13 The Self

13

How you perceive things in life, directly reflects the relationship you have with yourself.

#14 Self-awareness

14

You can only meet another person, as deeply as
you have met yourself.

#15 Duality

It is never 1 versus 2.
It is always 1 and 2.
Duality exists in polar opposites.

#16 Voice

16

Your responsibility in your human existence is to find your voice; because that is your one truly unique contribution to the world.

#17 Synchronicity

17

Synchronicity is the most powerful force within
the universe.

#18 Knowing

18

The more you know, the more you realize
nothing - and that is the point.

#19 Pain

You cannot experience ultimate pleasure without experiencing ultimate pain.

#20 Chaos

Diversity is created by chaos.
We are the only living beings able to create
beauty out of chaos.

#21 Healing

21

The only way out,
is through.